**BOTTOM DOG PRESS**

# ECHO

## POEMS

*Diana—*
*It's all good! Write*
*your own history—you*
*have the talent!*
*Christina*

~~Christina Lovin~~
Christina Lovin
Arnow Conference
April 11, 2014

HARMONY SERIES
BOTTOM DOG PRESS
HURON, OHIO

ISBN 978-1-933964-80-5

Bottom Dog Publishing
PO Box 425, Huron, Ohio 44839
http://smithdocs.net
e-mail: Lsmithdog@smithdocs.net

General Editor: Larry Smith
Layout & Cover Design: Susanna Sharp-Schwacke

## ACKNOWLEDGMENTS FOR *ECHO*

Poems in *Echo* have appeared in some form in the following journals
and anthologies

"A Cup of White Sugar"*, *Cold Shoulders, Evil Eyes* (Wising Up Press);
"Answering Myself," *Ruminate*; "Assumptions of the Virgin," *Poemeleon*
and *under/current*; "A Star Fell on Alabama," *Alehouse*; "A Tooth for a
Tooth," *Ab Ovo*; "Barefoot," *Feile Festa*; "Bridge," *Ayris* (published as
"Extraction"); "Brushing My Mother's Teeth," *Stimulus Respond*; "Burning
Love," *Carried Away* and *Poetry Quarterly*; "Candy Girl"*, *Escape Into Life*;
"Cry Babies"*, *Naugatuck River Review*; "Dedicated to the One I Love,"
*OVS Journal*; "Dog Star"*, *Carried Away* and *Poetry Quarterly*; "Echo I"*,
*Conclave: A Journal of Character*; "Echo II"*, *Conclave: A Journal of Character*;
"Echo Finds Her Voice," *Cliterature*; "Elegy for Sally and Rose," *Not a
Muse* (Haven Books, Hong Kong); "Elms," *Extinguished and Extinct*;
"Fledge," *Anthology of Appalachian Writers: Silas House Edition*; "Flesh"*,
*Cold Shoulders, Evil Eyes* (Wising Up Press); "Flipside," *Escape Into Life*;
"French Seams," *Naugatuck River Review*; "Future Secretaries of America,"
*Alehouse*; "Gathering Eggs"*, *Shakespeare's Monkey*; "Girl in the Red Hat"*,
*Poet Lore* and *Eating Her Wedding Dress* (Ragged Sky Press); "Haiku for a
Wanted Child," *Multi-Culti Mixerations*; "I Fall to Pieces"*, *Alehouse* &
*Escape Into Life*; "Lithophagus," *Stimulus Respond*; "Love Bite," *Carried
Away & Poetry Quarterly*; "Lunar Eclipse," *Escape Into Life*; "Many Ways
of Leaving," *Stimulus Respond*; "Mary's Child"*, *Not a Muse* (Haven Books,
Hong Kong);

ACKNOWLEDGMENTS continued on page 111

# TABLE OF CONTENTS

For Clara, my mother.
For my daughters, Brittany & Shannon.
For their daughters, Kira, Aracely, & Adriana,
& theirs to come.

*A little girl! Now ain't that the berries?!*—My mother, at my birth.

# Echo I

*We are the echo of the future...*—W. S. Merwin

# Echo I

## August 1960

Prairie town: hot August nights
when the corn with its narrow spaces
like confessionals can hide a girl
who wants to share the cool green secrets
and learn the names
of all things dark and wild. Who talks

with the incessant chat of crickets, talks
to the deepness between the rows of night.
And she can hear the whispered secrets
across the empty spaces
of the midnight house. Names
she can make out—the girl's

brothers, their many girlish
wives, dozens of children. Bad marriages: talk
of divorce, abuse, prison. Murderous secrets
to be hauled out and interrogated through the night
in those vacant spaces
between dusk and dawn. Named,

her mother's tears—her father's hot names
for fury and rage. Listen—you will be the girl
to witness and fill in the blank spaces
and you will tell all—you will talk
to the hollow halls of night
between the rows of corn in its secret

field and divulge the secrets
of being young, back when you learned the names
of stars that shone like truth in the night
sky, lying on a blanket in the blackness: a girl
and her father, talking
in the dark of outer space,

of how a large balloon can rise and travel the spaces
above the earth: those shining secrets
of Mylar and gasses. How you talked
together of the satellite's name,

which he couldn't remember—a girl's
maybe? But the names for midnight

you never spoke—nights appointed *shame, silence, secret*—
while together you watched *Echo* arc across dark space, named
for that girl who said too much—who learned it's better
            not to talk.

## WHERE THINGS CAME FROM

Summer. It seemed always
summer—hot wind driving
east from the prairies, heavy

with rain that refused to fall
to earth until it struck out
like a black snake poked one time

too many with a sharp stick,
the warning reverberations
ignored. Then slanting sheets

dropped and needles of rain
punctured the cinder dust,
stirring up that dark scent

of thirsty earth and water.
Mother lugged a washtub
to the corner of the house

beneath the gushing eaves,
to gather sweet rainwater
for the garden and the wash

while I splashed knee-deep in ditches.
But mostly it was hot. Sticky
tar boiled up black and tacky

between the lumps of limestone
gravel cast across the road,
tar that reeked of crude and burned

the feet of little barefoot girls
who dared to cross the heat
to feed the flock of neighbor's

lambs and rub their oily heads.
Sometimes a rock would shine
like gold and hold the shadow

of a bone or fin, some tiny life
etched against the face of stone.
Then August came again.

I'd meant to ask how fishes
pressed their feathered tails to mud
a hundred million years ago

and turned to tar, then stone.
My mother pulled brown paper
sacks over my feet and snapped

tan rubber bands around my
bony shins to hold the bags
in place. I tramped once more

across the gummy road to find
the meadow empty. Returned
to mother humming at the stove

as she had done each night
of my young life—the floor mopped,
the garden picked, fresh rye

bread on the board. This I ate,
refused the liver, and never
did I ask about the lambs.

## GIRL IN THE RED HAT

She wore red shoes, the girl in a red hat and nothing else.
I found her beautiful, released her from the thick sheaf
of artfully nude photographs in rather prim poses—
my father's samples for calendars he sold to be pinned
to the walls of men's clubs, auto shops, and back rooms
of bars. I nailed her to the wall of the chicken shed, admired
her creamy flesh, the color of a Rhode Island Red egg.
She dimpled at her hips and cheeks and knees, blushed
where rosy nipples bloomed from behind the proper slope
of those precise globes of her breasts. She was flawless but
for the harsh creases that ran the width and length of the print
where it had been folded to make her fit with her sisters
inside the sample case, her perfection spoiled with crackling ink,
crow's feet of the slick white paper beneath revealed.
Over and over I ran my palm across the paper, the wallboards
of the henhouse rough beneath my hand, futilely trying
to smooth her wrinkled skin, that crazing paper smile.

## GATHERING EGGS

The henhouse like any cathedral
nave—cool and hushed—
the old biddies muttering
at their stations. The cross
beams above lifting the vesper
chorus of pullets to the roof—
safe from the black snake
that lives beneath
the stone foundation.

I kneel before the congregation
of setters, one to a box,
collect the reluctant offerings
from beneath each warm
body, accept the blood
blisters kissed onto tender skin
as the price of obedience.

A single egg—the sacrifice
of a small, pale world
broken against the rough floor
of the henhouse—golden
stigmata that stains, then dries,
returning dust to dust.
A novice and her litany
of loss: too many eggs,
one old basket.

## SUNDAY

Baptized today, saved from her sin
by Jesus' blood and city water
at the front of the church in view of everyone.

Back home from church just in time to find
her father with a fat white hen in hand—
the blood, the blood, the crimson flood.

White feathers strewn around the yard,
dark stains across her pleated skirt
that would never wash clean again.

# CRY BABIES

My mother claimed she heard me crying a month before my birth—
squatted in the fresh-tilled garden plot beneath the thin scrim
of April clouds, cupping a handful of wrinkled lima beans,
her face close to her swollen belly, she swore she heard some
muffled keening from deep within herself—the impossible
unsound science of voice in a vacuum. There is a knowing
that transcends fact—begun in the womb or smacked into this world—
it was true. I was a crybaby. But I chose my sobs

like my father said to choose my battles: crying in my bed
for nights when his big black Chevy ran over my yellow kitten
as I watched from a spindled kitchen chair at the back screen door
while mother brushed my hair and that bit of sunshine chased shadows
beneath the trees across the drive, then writhed in death. Dying together
in a fiery crash, my favorite aunt and uncle left me consumed with quiet
sobs, but I bawled like a bottle calf on Papa's lap when he sang
"Daddy's Little Girl," weeping, I guess, because I was and always would be.

Nothing worse for a girl than dissolving into tears at a taunt
or jibe from a big brother or that freckled boy in the next desk.
His name escapes, the tears did not. The familiar pain would stricture
my chest like the remembrance of some strange, work-rough hand
squeezing my budding breast as we walked between tall rows of July corn,
ripe tassels dusting the top of my head, the sharp knowledge
of those rasping leaves cutting into bare skin and leaving scratches
as fingernails might, the scars deeper. I never learned to swallow my tears

like some girls do: hot-eyed but stoic the granddaughters of Him
of the cornfield whispered of a sin that rustled like cornstalks in the dark
as the three of us crowded a farmhouse bedroom one sultry summer night.
I began to understand that there are things to make a young girl cry,
things worse than being pinched or teased, things that begin with touch,
with squeeze, but end where I would not go for ten years with sweat and groan—
things that ruin, that instruct a child in the meanings of words like *taint,*
*besmirch, sully,* and *defile*: that naming of darkness and its deepest silence.

# THE OTHER SISTER

*At 18 weeks, fingerprints have begun to form, from this point on, every individual can be uniquely identified.*
> —Placard on 18-week embryo at the Life &
> Genetics Exhibit, Museum of Science and
> Industry, Chicago

I will always remember
as I did then at twelve—naïve child
stunned by human embryos
in tall glass canisters shelved and on display
at the museum. A school girl thrilled:
tiny shivers at the horror of death,
a throbbing buzz of expectancy.
My own body beginning to bud—
those concentric circles of life
present inside me before my birth—
my latent offspring secure within
my ovaries—as we were in our mother's:
me and she. Waiting together
for mother's release, our father's life spark —
she, the older sister, going first,
trying hard; her tenuous hold loosing.

I have heard it told how sometimes in Mexico
a large jar is passed around a village,
a lifeless fetus inside, curled pink
and meaty as fresh sausage at the bottom,
displayed to family, neighbors,
anyone who will look—the curious,
the sympathetic, and those who understand
the need to declare, to not forget:
*Este es mi niño,* "This is my child."
And back in time, I see again
those urns—obscene glass bellies
filled with the grotesque unborn
in their stages of growth—tiny blob
of flesh, flat-eyed fish, a gilled tadpole,
some tiny monkey complete with tail,
burgeoning humans—each someone's.

Eighteen weeks, with fingerprints
whorled like intricate maps to where
she disappeared, who she might have become,
my sister's leaving made room for me.
From that point on, I believe
I would have known her anywhere.

### FLASH FLOOD:
### KNOX COUNTY, ILLINOIS
### 1959

I remember a long hill
down to a wooden crossing,
a small gray trailer overturned
sideways to the roaring creek.
Dark sky, empty arms
of October oaks.

Two days the girl lay
covered with a blanket
of whorled leaves:
white flower bud
of her small fist
all that was visible
when the weeping men,
my father among them,
came upon her.

What I didn't witness,
what I did: little home
of no one I knew,
empty house
never entered again.

# SHELLS

My father once took us to a cottage by the Mississippi—
my mother, my youngest brother, two or more
of an older brother's children—their parents fighting
again, or divorced by then: another sister-in-law
to disappear, the promise of a new one on the air.

The weather was cool—the river below lethargic,
clinging with frozen fingertips to the impassive shore
while we shivered at night in the corners of the cabin,
stringing shells, callously emptied of snails, on leather laces
to wear like natives under striped blankets hung
over clothesline—a thin cord that split the rafters' spaces.

By day, sunlight spread thin as ice on the path to the shore.
We walked to stay warm toward Oquawka, past a crossroads
I remember well. Pines gossiped coldly, tall on all sides,
crowding the rutted roads where they crossed, littered
with ruined shells from the button factory, shells that filled
low places in the road: opalescent pink, creamy and smooth

as flesh. Muscle and meat of clams once clung there,
secluded in their rough armor like young girls' hearts
can be. Punched with holes—any usefulness
in the parts taken away, blank-faced until carved
and shot through, pierced and sewn to hearts
of strangers—cast-off shells lay broken underfoot.

## FLESH

Back when everything was black and white
and even crayons had a voice
of politics and race,
art class should have been our favorite,
spoiled only by a teacher we students loathed:
her built-up shoe and leg brace emblems
of survival, her crutch a weapon
in her private war against expression
by children who wished to defy her demand:

"Make the heads the size of a grapefruit!"
Resulting in hydrocephalic figures
crowded together on rough sheets
of cheap art paper,
their bodies floating below
those cranial balloons
like kite tails made from arms and legs
and skeletal torsos.

Households of folks
with similar inflated features,
schoolyards of distended skulls at play,
toting along their appendages
like afterthoughts or unwanted offspring,
all colored from the same 48-crayon Crayola box,
all colored the same color: *Flesh*.

Even by the polite *colored* children
and the Garza's, whose eyes were bright
*Black*, whose warm skin was close to *Indian Red*.
The only Indians we knew
were in TV westerns on Saturday night
and Saturday morning *Andy's Gang* jungle flicks,
portrayed in light and dark
tones of gray by actors in pancake makeup;
even African tribesmen
carrying their fearsome spears
and shields were played by white men.

The Swede children—Anderson, Ericson,
Johnson, and Swanson—chose *Periwinkle*
or *Cornflower* for their eyes;
the German's, David and Anne,
*Prussian Blue* or simple *Brown.*
The teacher frowned, her horn
rims' glass glaring at children
who dared to choose *Burnt Sienna*
or *Sepia* to color the faces and arms and hands
of their bulging-mugged families.

When we were finished,
small fingers smelled of paraffin
and the waxy colors were replaced
side-by-side back inside their boxes.
All around the chalk-dusted classroom
rectangles floated, taped against blackboards
and crowded with over-sized noggins,
their superfluous, atrophied bodies,
and even a school kid could see
that things were terribly out of proportion.

# A CUP OF WHITE SUGAR

In the fifties, in my town, on my street,
segregation was a word
we didn't know. At least in my house. Not me:
my mother would send me to the neighbor's
for a loaf of bread, some lard, a cup of white
flour or sugar, weekly if not more. Mrs. Gatlin

(Florence I would come to know later)
was gentle and kind, offering me
on every visit a piece of ribbon candy:
swirling colors—red, yellow, green—against white
satiny sweetness, stretched, then swirled
back onto themselves over and over again.

Her house, like her, was neat and dark
and smelled of pork hocks and greens,
cornbread in iron skillets. Her daughter,
a princess in pink chiffon and white
lace-trimmed anklets with shiny black
Mary Janes. Her sons, shadowy

twins to my brothers. We children of the same
block of unpaved streets and ditches
filled with weeds and empty liquor
bottles played side by side until
one dark boy and I joined in a game
of Cowboys and Indians. Mrs. Gatlin saw us—

him patting me down to check for six-shooters
or knives, as I lay prone in the grass, felled
by an imaginary bullet: a scenario played out
every Saturday of our young lives
on the TV westerns all we children watched,
where white gunmen shot the bad guys,

Mexicans outlaws, or the ubiquitous
Indians. She must have told my mother.
Duane and I never played together again.
I couldn't understand. All the while
I rode my old, blind horse past thin-walled
shanties at the end of the street far from ours

(the only white house on Pennsylvania),
where the black-tarred road met Knox and rutted yards
of skinny children played in the mud, stopping
only to squeal and point at me. And my father
brought deer meat—road-killed, processed,
and wrapped in thick white paper—to people

happy to get it. Unrest burned holes in the summer
nights miles from there, and my mother spoke
of a somber darkness outside the back door
of the diner she and my father had run up on Grand,
where our very neighbors would wait
in the shadows for their orders. Not coming in

so as "not to shame you, Mizz Ericson."
Soon enough I would stand again, impatient,
oblivious child, in that clean dim living room
while Mrs. Gatlin fetched a cup of white
sugar from her fragrant kitchen and placed
in my pale, open hand that bright, twisted candy.

# ELMS

In memory of the Lombard Elm, 1868-1965

## I.

Elms graced the white-lined streets of town
like timeworn widows or those old maids found
at church potlucks at Lincoln Park—elegant
but outdated, their feathered hats a quiver
with gossip and gospel, their sturdy arms
full of pies, fried chicken, and green gelatin
thick with canned pear halves, walnuts,
and Jesus. Out there where the black-faced
statues of deferential jockeys lined white-rock
lanes around the park. Expectantly, they bowed
beneath the elms every fifty feet, hands held out
as if to hold the reins of some rich man's horse,
or gather a penny tip, then diffidently dip
their heads to murmur, "Yassir." Some statues
stood guard at the dark pond where small
bright fish and larger black fish struggled
for breath together among the choking
water lilies. They attended the white-painted
bandstand set among imposing centenary elms.
They were just a part of the park. Less interesting
than the forlorn bear cage where we pale children
played tag and peered down through iron bars
at the dim dungeon below. Decades before
it had held some sad, chained animal. Black children—
some I knew from school—squealed and ran
in and out of the turbid water along a strip
of rocky, gritty beach, glimpsed only from a rowboat
rented from our side, on the far shore of the lake.

## II.

Elm Town was ignorant of what was and what was
to come: the first diseased tree discovered
on a boulevard near the center of town, where old elms
gathered around the even older college, an aging family
of still virile gentlemen whose wizened faces
seemed to peer into the future and see what lay

there—inevitable, yet unfathomable. Polio,
too, threatened—a thing too small to see, yet larger
than life itself when viewed through a mirror
attached to an iron lung. So my father took us
three Sabin Sundays to stand in long lines
in the gymnasium, black and white waiting together
for the cure soaked into sugar cubes like the squares
my father brought me from hotels in Chicago
or Peoria, wrapped neatly in fine paper, tucked
into his leather valise. We swallowed the bitter-
sweet remedy, despised the taint of medicine,
while outside in the Lombard yard, the giant elm
(*second largest in the country*)—breathed
in our useless breaths, returning the life-
giving oxygen—stood tall, still vibrant
at ninety. Soon, Old Ben would fall
to the epidemic, the DDT-cure ineffective
and dangerous. Unmindful, we walked out
into a town of ten thousand elm trees
spreading their strong summer canopies of green
over the streets, their shadows dappling
the oblivious brick that, too, would soon be gone,
obliterated beneath a smothering caul of asphalt.

## POUND

My brothers would go there to shoot the rats
that ravaged the bodies of dead strays
laid out in trenches like those I'd seen before
in pictures of Auschwitz—deep ruts spanning
the property's width behind the small cinder
block building that housed the living,

waiting animals. Once, a small black bear
paced in circles in one of the cages.
My father took me there again to choose
a kitten, my own dead beneath the wheels
of his car. And once, my bicycle crunched
up the gravel drive past the kennels,
to the back of the building, where two men
in dark uniforms waited beside a truck,
a dog-sized metal box resting in the bed.
Rubber tubing ran from the closed box
to the exhaust. The engine whined softly
as the driver leaned against the fender,
smoking a Camel. Howls of laughter from
both men—a joke about something. Crushing

his smoke with his boot heel, one turned and barked
"Go home. This ain't no place for a girl." Later,
when the pound had been left to the lost
and abandoned, I returned to search
the twilight ditches for that certain dog—
impossible in the piles upon piles
of furred bodies—those that were still,
and those others darting darkly among them.

## DOG STAR

Sputnik II, November 4, 1957

*The more time passes, the more I'm sorry....*
*We shouldn't have done it....*
   —Oleg Gazenko, Russian Space Scientist in
   2002


Little stray, small vagabond safe on the streets
of Moscow, how did they lure you from doggy ways:
nosing through trash, days of begging in the square,
nights curled up tight in corners, under porches,
stretching in the morning to begin again
with those bright eyes? You came to love them,

your captors: how a dog trusts with her eyes
and her tail and her huge, huge heart: *Laika*—
Little Barker, Little Curly—*Krudyavka, Limonchik*—
Little Lemon, *Zhuchka* —Little Bug: diminutives
for betrayal, for cruelty, for small, smaller,
and yet smaller spaces, until you learned
not even to defecate or urinate, and ate
what they fed you—disgusting gel—all that
you were given. Breathed only what they allowed,
panting in panic, your pulse a race no one would win.

To the end sure that the one with the kind voice
and tender hands would come to rescue you
from that screaming capsule, the intense airless heat,
from your anguished hell in the heavens. Would come
and release the chafing harness catches, lift you
from the shell, remove the electrodes that stung
and itched, gently rub your singed ears, seared
belly. Call you again *good dog, khoroshaya sobaka.*

But no intention of rescue—no way of return
from your unfortunate orbit. Only lies as all men
provide in such situations: claiming you died
peacefully, while we children of earth witnessed you
trail across the awful darkness in your brilliant death.

## YOUR LIFETIME IN PICTURES

When I was too young to read all the words, I learned the world
page by page—black and white photographs of what seemed important
to remember in 1955—*Your Lifetime in Pictures.*
Hard enough to remember back then to my own little life.
For there are memories sometimes more real than my own—

the world captured and captioned in "2,000 pictures"—
the first that of a mushroom cloud mounting up from the ocean—
ships dwarfed by the rising plume, writhing palm trees recoiled
along the shore. "World-shaping" the caption reads, as if a choice
were being made somewhere as someone pushed that button. As if

an entire universe was not just then expanding inside
a dim living room outside the city limits of small town
Illinois, between the small ears of she who was me—
that little barefoot girl in braids and jeans, my own flat atlas
of the past spread open on my lap: I don't remember

the first time the cover was laid back, but what I first learned
of death through the camera's open eye, I do: page 23
and the "Defeat of Russia"—the Russians lay where they fell,
some trying to rise, others—a woman and young girl—seeming
to outrun the bullets from unseen guns. What held me

spellbound was not life, however, but death—dead bodies
on every continent, in every imaginable way: corpses
in pomp—the Pope lying in state like a benign Santa Claus—
massacred troops broken open by bombs and bullets,
frozen stiffly as dolls on the battle field, gassed Jews

and gypsies in Germany and Poland, the Hindenburg in flames,
the serene last portrait of Anastasia and her doomed family—
unimaginable to me then, but soon I would understand,
our own small table circled with empty chairs and grief. My training
for death crowded my dreams and nightmares: images

of the "Jap" soldiers who "still preferred death to surrender"
on page 186—the toe of the one still pressing the trigger of his gun,
half his face blown away. In sleep, I became the little girl pulled dead
from a well, my body wrapped in a blanket, hauled up by weeping men;
I feared the dark for years after. This was my lifetime before I even had a life—

disaster, crime, war, scandal—our own and the world's. But childish
hope, too. For the last photograph is that of a Minnesota girl
born without arms—a pretty teen, she holds a pencil between her toes,
leaning forward to balance, with great concentration, she writes. She *writes*.

## Echo II

*Like a daughter in a legend, I had been somewhere else....I had broken the spell of place and family.*

—Eavon Boland

## LAUNDRY

Father's khaki work shirts saluted
to the state in rows like an army
of masculinity: tan generals and pale privates
rose to attention with each gust of wind
that rubbed soft in summer the rows
of robust denim, froze them in winter
(they came in to sulk alone, rigid
as religion, beside the furnace grate)
while the boys danced impatiently,
wanting so much to be gone.

My own clothes, hand-sewn of material
stored in the attic for decades—
feed sack prints and out of date fabrics—
seersucker, dotted Swiss, dimity,
and chintz—tossed petulantly
among my mother's simple frocks.

I once found her written words
in a cloth-covered notebook:
heartfelt prayers for her children:
blessings and absolutions
spelled out beside each name
in that familiar squared hand.

She taught me to write: ABC's
pressed with lead into cheap paper.
I copied each stroke, every camber
and closed arc, over and over again,
her clear script becoming mine—
my name a span of homemade letters
that fluttered and waved across the page,
pinned to the lines like rumpled laundry—

symbols of who I might become, who I was
back then. I looked down from the attic
window to my unwritten life, a blank
expanse of sheets, bleached clean by the sun,
rising and falling like deep, slow breaths
of sleep, as if alive with a daughter's dreams.

### Brushing My Mother's Teeth

Not what you might think. Not those
I remember only from photos
of a gap-toothed young woman.

Solid, these are held in my hand: soiled—
yellow and caked with starch from nursing
home food. The brush sends out specks that stick

to the faucet, spot the break-proof mirror
in the tiny shared toilet. Another woman
mumbles incoherently on the other side

of the cheap laminate door while water runs
clear now around the precise shape
of my mother's shrunken gums, sloughing

the smooth channel, rinsing clean each tooth,
perfect save for the chip hewn from the left front
incisor; and I remember her foot—

wet, dripping warm, scented
water back into an enamel basin,
then gently rubbed, lovingly patted

dry to be followed by the other.
The foot washer rising, untying
the long linen towel kept just for this

sacred observance. I see my mother accept the cloth,
winding it around her waist, then kneel
before the next woman in the circle.

Takes her foot, lifts it by a callused heel
into the washbowl between them.
I watch bored, too young to participate,

not understanding then those offices of humility
one will stoop to out of duty or tradition,
and on occasion, some reverent love.

## BAREFOOT

I remember that year I had only the red shoes
to wear to school. I learned to hate shoes then, embarrassed
by scarlet t-straps clashing with my pink angora or blue
mohair, just so brother could go to college. *Capezios-*
to-match cost money and money was scarce as daylight
had been in windowless shanties beside the mud runnels
of Barefoot Nation, Illinois. Mother told me about Barefoot:
impoverished immigrant Irish sharing one pair of shoes
in each family of many-sized feet. Only one at a time
could venture to town, walking the ten rutted miles
in boots too small to lace, or strapped with baling twine
to stop them from dropping off. I was a vain child
then. What did I care of the dead who need no shoes?
Now I see my arch is high and proud. Like hers. Like theirs.

# FRENCH SEAMS

Seventh Grade Home Economics: thirty girls
in a space half kitchen-half sewing room,
we prepared for our lives as wives.
How little we knew; how much less we learned.

We burned the toast, boiled over the water
for rubbery poached eggs, covered in clabbered
Hollandaise. Labored over creation
of simple aprons—skills that would serve
us well in our future roles as our mothers' daughters.

The stitching all wrong on mine—awkward
gathers clumped together like tight groups
of gossiping girls, the gleaming
threads of their hair tangled together
as they leaned close, scornful as needles
pricking the flesh of a bare finger.

Trying to rip out those bunched stitches,
I tore a long gash— my apron in two
unequal pieces, hanging by a frayed thread.
I cried to teacher—wanting perfection,
wanting to be good as a future homemaker.

She mothered us like a big sister—the closest
thing to children she would have—
showed me how to tear the thin fabric apart:
three nearly equal parts sewn together,
folded over, then joined again with graceful seams
against the tiny rosebuds and vines.

My apron earned an A. I took it home
to show my mother, where she peeled
the last of a five-pound bag of potatoes,
watched over a pot of steaming greens.

The wrong side of town, where
cheap cuts of pork sizzled in lard
for supper. Where my father deserved
the largest piece of crisp meat,
where my brothers fought me for the rest.

Across town, teacher sat down to a light meal
of savory Welsh rarebit and a green salad
with fresh Russian dressing. For dessert,
Charlotte Russe (just a bit!) and coffee, no sugar.

Warm light from a perfect sunset fell
across crystal, silver, the china she had chosen
for herself, and her grandmother's tablecloth—
fragile lace pieced together with skillful stitches
in French seams—on a table set perfectly for one.

## OLD MAIDS

Crisp autumn nights, they lay alone
at the bottom of the bowl—
some blackened, some still golden
but singed around the edges:
unmet potential of bursting
into something other
than those un-popped
kernels tossed out
onto the frigid beds
of last summer's bachelor's buttons.

## Two Sijo

### Future Secretaries of America

In typing class they sat in rows,
fingers floating above cold keys.

Every girl's head bent to the right
waiting to be told when to start.

No quick brown foxes sly enough
to see the lazy dogs ahead.

### Damn You, Barbie #1

Too old for dolls, I still had asked:
That leggy blonde with tiny waist.

The bitch would always make me feel
too short, dark, and never enough.

That one I couldn't give away:
she taunts me still from her cardboard hell.

## Paper Doll Ghazal

When she was ten, she had a shoebox full of tatty dolls
with painted tag board faces—creased and worn out shabby dolls.

She loved Elizabeth Taylor the most—those violet eyes
and small waist a far cry from her buggy full of chubby dolls.

Kim Novak had a blonde mystique about her quiet face—
sultry in pajamas— ruffled pink paper baby dolls.

Coquettish Debbie Reynolds smiled the widest of them all.
Why not? She hauled in Eddie Fisher—that hunky hubby-doll!

Betty Davis must have been a hand-me-down: the cousins'
boxes of outgrown clothes each fall sometimes held a grubby doll.

When seasons changed, there was no Bloomingdales for paper girls—
no mall—Sears catalog gave hope for all but snobby dolls.

Swimsuits painted on, they couldn't change. But Chris donned a bra
and a cardboard smile stiff as any other unhappy doll's.

## To the Ghosts of Halloween

When children could go out
alone, unafraid
of strangers, I remember a scarecrow
and my brother as a mountain
man in trap-door long johns
and a long red beard.

Once he was an African
bushman—all black face, wide smile
painted in white, long grasses
circling his waist. A spear in hand,
he showed no shame
at the doors
of our black neighbors.

Later, he and his friend
would take two costumes—change
at the end of the block to return
like sleazy politicians
with different faces
at the houses with the best treats.

When my foot was bandaged
from a surgery and sutures,
I was Red Riding Hood: hooded
red winter coat, my pillowcase
heavy when I came limping home,
red rubber boots full of blood.

I was a clown when I was ten—
red and white striped
pajamas my mother had sewn
from heavy flannel I would
wear all that coming winter
when cold settled in my attic room.

And then the bride: my vision
blurred by the veil of the bedroom
curtain's lace hanging over my eyes,
obscuring where I would go
with my stumbling steps
in that costume I would one day wear,
then tear off like so many useless rags.

## Two Sijo II

### Roller Rink on a Saturday Night

Spinning around that oval rink,
the music's pull like gravity:

orbiting like a satellite
a girl can become quite dizzy,

hormones fueling the teenage stars
from apogee to perigee.

### *The Lombard Echo* 1963

On glossy page—September smiles
belying our uncertainties—

we're pictured there in black and white,
as history is often viewed:

not knowing then that fall would turn
as November's cold turned bitter.

## ECHO II

### January 1964

Sometimes it's wise to do a thing
twice—like kiss that certain boy when we left the dance
at Teen Town and crossed the dim
street to the garage of the dry cleaners, where
we were not the only ones making out
in the dark, shivering in the freezing January silence.

The bulky forms of trucks, stolid and silent,
seemed disapproving as a girl's father; but couples did their thing—
first base, mostly, a few more daring, and where
his shaking fingers brushed my chest, I felt a dance
of nerves and heat, my breath let out
in sharp puffs of white that disappeared into the dim

gloom. Back on the dance floor, the lights were dimming,
while the Beach Boys crooned "Surfer Girl," and boys silenced
girls with kisses in the snack shop booths where
they could not be seen and could hide that something
bulging in their Levis under the tables. They might dance
a finger along a white thigh, bared by an out-

grown skirt or one that was rolled at the waistband once out-
side the house and mother's view. Bad girls might slide a hand under the dim
table or hook her fingers in a boy's belt loops when they danced,
fingers fanned across his denim ass. Good girls box-stepped in silence
as they'd been taught after school in Social Dance Club—something
that girls like me never learned—too dark, too awkward, coming from where

the end of town met the edge of the sticks. Not like girls who lived where
the houses stood aloof and distant as wallflowers, or out
at the lake and country club, their sun-lightened hair gleaming like something
precious. Even in the winter. Even in the dimmest
corner of Teen Town in the basement of the YMCA, where they silently
shuffled right-back, left-over, right-together, left-forward, right-together, a dance

they were just beginning to learn: that rigid dance
of boy and girl, then man and woman, then give and give and take and take, where
good girls married lawyers or doctors and learned the moves of silence,
boxed into lock-steps that went nowhere and provided no way out.
Me? I never really learned to dance, but wedged into a corner of that dim
garage on a narrow side street in Small Town, USA, something


moved me to kiss that boy a second time. Something
            that would often lead me back to where
I can't return: the bass's dull beat echoing up from the dim
            basement of the Y as we walked out
into the January night, while above us a dancing dot of light
            boogied across the sky in utter silence.

## PRINCESS

My father knew best: he never called me
*Kitten* or *Princess*. But every girl deserves
a tiara at least once in her life, doesn't she?
Grace Kelly had hers twice: the roles of a lifetime—
princess in *The Swan*, then that real-life prince
who carried her away to his kingdom by the sea.
While Cinderella made it good—rags to riches—
and Snow White got an awakening from a kiss,
Lee Meriwether waved her gloved hand
and smiled down that long runway as Burt sang:

"There she is…" And there I was at seven:
a white sweatshirt stretched over my chubbiness,
my hair a crown of dark brown with gold-
red glints, and across my flat little chest
in my mother's best embroidered stitches:
*Miss America 1967*: eleven years to wait
and primp, preparing to be a queen. Only to find
myself hesitation-stepping down some narrow June
aisle, too young, too stupid in my own coronet
of pearls. Eager to kiss the frog at the altar,
who would never transform into a prince.

## SUMMER '68

For the boys who did not return and the girls
who waited

How strong the young bulls in their summer fields;
how rare the blood-red steaks upon our plates
at backyard barbecues. For summer yields
those lingering kisses at the station gates,

where sons and brothers, heading off to war,
press promises to the ears of stoic girls,
who, red-eyed, turn away and pass through doors
that open to their safe, familiar worlds.

How sweet those worlds of elm and maple trees
that line the brick-paved streets of sleepy towns,

and march along the lanes of cemeteries'
rows of stones, bare and tortured new-turned ground.

The grass will grow, another spring will yield
fresh herds of young calves running through the fields.

## BRIDGE

In the dentist's chair, a gape
between my molars awaiting
a bridge to recreate my smile,
I am high on nitrous oxide.
Or did the assistant just say
that? Am I? I am? Is that
an earphone in my ear
or is it an angel? Emmy Lou
Harris is singing "The Boxer," and I lose
my equilibrium in the whirling
of my brain. It should be someone
else whose name I can't remember
just now. Simone? Nina Simone?
No. Garfinkel? Garfunkel?
Simon and Garfunkel. *Yes*.

Emmy Lou sings on: "Li-la-li,
li-la-li li, li,li, li." I'm lying
in this chair, afloat in her voice.
Drifting on her raw, urgent voice
with no paddle up my canoe.
*Is that right?* No, Christina.
The assistant says something.
"I was just waiting for someone
like you," Emmy sings. I open my mouth

and nod as if knowing what was asked.
The good patient. But I am not
in this chair, I am rising above
the student center at my old college,
where the steps are littered with leaves—
gold, red, brown. "Good times
and lovers..." In the mist, the old main
building remains, standing stately
on the corner across the quad
in gray stone and dim hallways
where it was torn down
in '68, and we live down the block
and I am young again. All of us

are still alive. "I've grown used to losing,"
Emmy croons, "what I'm fondest of."
I think of boys I knew there—
never more than friendly
strangers, but returning to me
now in this numb fog of pleasure
and pain. Three brothers, dead
for years now. My mother, father,
friends. That girl down the hall

who was killed my freshman year.
Her room as empty as her parents' faces
when they came to gather her belongings.
I don't want to remember what I am
in this state: I've gone inside
the student center, down the stairs,
or is it up from the basement?
I don't know now—the sun is glinting
in from the snow outside the tall,
tall windows in sharp shards of light.
Does that building even exist? Do I?

*Are you all right?* The assistant whispers
and pats my shoulder. *The work
is finished.* She's said this,
not me. I nod and open my eyes
as if I understood the words.
As if floating, lost on this current
of time and drowning in the past
with no bridge in sight, I care.

## A Tooth for a Tooth

In my sewing box, mate-less buttons, halves
of snaps, hooks with no eyes, and a tooth
rattle around together. Gone now, all my wisdom
teeth. Pulled and discarded, except for this one—
shaped like the letter *J* and brutish, a fossilized
tusk, something beastly from out a primeval jowl
it would seem—the prize from an archeological dig.
But it is mine and I have kept it. And now, I find
I miss myself sometimes; there is an emptiness
in my jaw and a hole in my head. Several
to be sure: settings without the creamy pearls,
fiber, and pulp that were part of me.

My precious stones, forgive me: I'm taking all of you back—
impacted molar, cavity-ridden canine, chipped incisor.
That sliver, too, of sawn bone that worked itself out
of my jaw back some years ago. I worried
it with my tongue until it poked my gum,
but just when it emerged to where I could touch it
with my finger, I swallowed and it was lost. I want it
back now to hold you all in place, my teeth;
you who served me for so long, whole and firm until
pregnancy and illness leached calcium from my body
and we began to fall apart together.

Come back, my darling jewels, to the welcoming warmth
of my mouth. Come, broken as you have been
on sunflower seed, or crumbled by a nut, and you,
little gem of my own creation, stalagmite
of me, return in whatever shape you exist
from your graveyard of teeth. I conjure your emptiness
with my tongue. There are places for you
to fill. The others are lonely here
without you. We sing you back with the lisp
with which you left us.

# MARY'S CHILD

*I returned to find that my vocabulary of belonging was missing.*
                                        —Eavon Boland

## FLIP SIDE

Wherever she was
she wanted to be
elsewhere. She sat full
of distance and longing
for open road ahead and no cross
streets to slow for.
Doing, she longed for
undoing, as night fingers
the delicate catches of day's light
garment. Loosed,
her mind raced, escaped
the course never completed
and leapt the probable
into the realm of fools
and fallen women, falling
but never finding
foothold like seafarers
ashore, their legs unsteady
on terra firma. Wavering
reflection of her own face
in the lying mirror,
unfamiliar as the flip side
of some one-hit-wonder 45.

## DEDICATED TO THE ONE I LOVE

For the 60s girl groups

The clock radio of bubble gum pink plastic glowed
like some unknown desire in the dark
of her room, while it churned out its Silver
Dollar Survey of adolescent prophecies:
Today I met the boy I'm gonna marry.
I met him on a Monday. He's so fine. He's a rebel.
I'm just a foolish little girl. Then he kissed me
and that's why I fell for the leader of the pack.
The clock face throbbed like a broken-heart

or a school girl's blush as Dick Biondi sullied
the airwaves at WLS from Chicago
and Wolfman Jack howled across the country
while the girl groups ruled the airwaves.
Their words and melodies burrowed
into her brain as she slept with the radio
on. You can't hurry love, she would dream;
one fine day we'll be together. Mama said
there'd be days like this. They crooned

far into the night—Ronnie, Darlene, Mary
and the twins, Mary and Diana and Flo,
Mary by herself, Martha and the others:
those who, like a masked Greek chorus, lent
their rich, dark voices to so many unseen
groups their music rose like one tragic choir—
part gospel, part sin, all sex and sadness:
Chantals, Chiffons, Shirelles, Crystals.
Cupcakes, Cookies, Cakes, and Dixie Cups.

Please, Mr. Postman, stop in the name of love
and be my guy: be my, be my little baby.
In her dreams they congregated at the Chapel
of Love declaring my boyfriend's back
and there's gonna be trouble. And maybe
she lay in the dark listening
and telling herself: let Johnny get angry
because he hit me and it felt like a kiss.

In the heat lightning of passion and prairie
summer night the neighbor beat his wife
on the front lawn outside her bedroom window.
Oh no. Oh no. Oh no, no, no, no, no.
Only the stitches on his spouse's face,
the saving coagulation of her blood,
kept that fragile, tattered marriage
from ripping apart. For he was really good/
bad, not evil. Remember, life can never be exactly
what we want it to be. Will you still love me tomorrow?

Note: In 1961, the popular girl group, The Crystals, put out a single with the title
"He Hit Me and It Felt Like a Kiss." Carole King wrote the song (with Gerry
Goffin), reportedly after learning that singer Little Eva, (King's former babysitter)
was being beaten by her boyfriend. The song was pulled from radio play almost
immediately, but went on to be covered by Courtney Love's group, Hole, and
Amy Winehouse.

## Two Sijo III

### Candy Girl

We're all singing in harmony
dancing in step to the cha-cha

Our skirts are hiked up to minis
streaked hair ratted to the rafters

We're tough girls, smelling of stale smoke
Pep-O-Mint and sweet backseat sex

### Slow Burn

We lay on blankets at the lake
tanning until the sun went down

Shaking and baking in a smear
of baby oil and iodine

The smell of hot dogs filled the air
sizzling and crackling in their skins

## SOMEONE ELSE'S SIN

Sinner at seven, she begged for baptism—
plunged backward beneath the water
in a white robe at the front of the church

for God and all to witness. Her sins?
Those of the flesh. Her own. For when she told
of the rough touch, her mother said to pray

for *him*, while a tiny blaze ignited in her. Sinless
in dreams, a stranger on a train would fall
in love with her, his sandpaper hands squeezing

past the elastic band of her *Sunday* panties.
At twelve, she prayed to an unhearing God
that she would stop. A promise. At fifteen,

she pled for baptism once more, to wash away
completely her desire for timid kisses, the cloying breath
of lanky boys with Ipana smiles against her

cheek and Chapsticked lips as if—*forgive us
our trespasses*—those sweet-hot thoughts
that smoldered and smelted inside her
head and body might be someone else's sins.

## MARY'S CHILD

Sunday morning front row girl—
scrubbed clean of Saturday night's
back seat—pillboxed and pearled—
gloves, washed whiter than snow,
pulled tight to wrists, covering the crimson
fingernails and pink flesh beneath.

No virgin ever bore a daughter.
She is offspring of that other Mary—
the one who knew redemption
has no value but to the sinner;
that the willful, wandering lamb
becomes more precious
than the sheltered flock
to the watchful shepherd;
and the prodigal can only be
welcomed home when everything
has been lost in a far country.

And just yesterday—just last night—
just as she was—surrendered all
to this Sabbath-suited Lucifer
by her side. Who, taking her
to the top of the world, promised it
to her if she would kneel
down before him.

Now he stands Bible in hand—
head bowed reverently—
gazing into her
black patent leather shoes
reflecting on heavenly things
above.

## THE MOURNING AFTER

Small room of little death—full
flower of last night dropping
petals, delicate fern
casting short, fine, hairs
like those shorn from dark
and private places
across the bare table.

Two votives—breaths spent
together in shuddering
prayers—their molten
wax hard, now, beneath
the fingertips.

The crumpled bed is cold.
A small patch of blood—
heart shaped stigmata
spread across stiff white—
dried to the hue of *memento
mori* roses pressed long ago,
fragile edges falling away
at a touch.

## WHAT THE OTHER WOMAN KNOWS:
### HAIKU TO BE READ ALONE

Two bodies touching—
wet trails on hot summer skin,
the damp brush of leaves.

Eyelashes flicker—
a rush of wings when coming:
lost feathers, stirred air.

Unfold your pressed lips—
clean linen shakes on the line,
footfalls crush new grass.

Flame from used candles—
the memory of a color,
short wicked and blue.

Wilting like desire,
shot out towards summer's end—
loosestrife's lost flower.

Wounded stem to bud,
seeping on the window sill—
ripe peaches split wide.

The dove's unsigned notes—
three drops in an empty sink—
a single plate drips.

Oiled against the cold,
opening only inward—
one narrow doorway.

## Lunar Eclipse

At six the moon is rising in the east,
a red wound on the bruised brow
of the hill. The sun is setting, also red,
behind us in the West. As far apart

as two can be and still share that scoop
of blue above this earth. Tonight, the world

will come between them, cast devouring
shadows to the sky, blackening the eye
of night, the only glow remaining
the hope of foolish Venus in the dark.

## HALF TRUTHS

A myth of time
and measure: one second
more, one second less,
one extra grain of sand
beyond the bosom of the hour
glass, passing her slender waist,
filling that insatiable belly.

The crumpled form in swaddling
plastic. Rumor is her name,
expediency her fate.
Her final grave among the cast off
syringes, empty vials, still
she moves one tiny finger.

And clinging to the weaving
strap on the St. Charles line,
the uniform and apron
speak of halfway across town
from the Garden District,
no matter the glower, those shoes
and purse of defiant red.

## HAIKU FOR A WANTED CHILD

Conceived in winter:
in the cold room warm bodies
give mutual heat.

Like a gentle drift,
the pillow where you now rest
lifted my bare hips.

Your father's tantrums
when he learns of your coming
flash like silver sleet.

Our roof leaks badly,
but inside me you are safe
from cruel spring showers.

May, I lie alone
on half the vacant bed.
He is gone. You stayed.

Ripe summer belly
veined as a map of the earth,
globed atlas of hope.

Sweet breaking open—
my body an autumn fig
pressing out its seed.

Winter once again:
two bodies under old quilts,
each warms the other.

## ANSWERING MYSELF

The ring is distant—a bell
without its tongue—clucking
at the other end of the line—
then the rasp of machination—
an answering machine—
my own voice asking
for a message and a number.

*986.* The number
of miles from where I left
only to answer myself
over the startled receiver
so very far away.

I leave the message:
*Miles are only distance,*
*but time is clumsy,*
*a stupid thief—broken*
*hours fill my ears: listless*
*droning of bees in a time of drought.*
*Do you remember everything*
*I wasn't, all that we were,*
*before I called and you didn't*
*answer?*

        But I did,
as always, answering myself
with an unrequited question.

## LITHOPHAGUS

*Lithophagus: he not only swallowed flints...but such stones*
*as he could reduce to powder...which to him was a most*
*agreeable and wholesome food.*
                    —from *Forgotten English,* Jeffery Kacirk.

Guilty pleasures, stones. And laundry starch—hard tablets
that my mother chewed when pregnant with my brother,
who then, in turn, spooned the earth to eat the dirt
and sucked the grit and pebbles that remained. He savored
soil like some would relish wines or sweets. Perhaps he knew
the richest corner of the yard and where to dig
to find the finest loams or piquant marls where roots
of grass grasped silica and grubs had left their shit.

It must be a legacy: this family trait, this brittle
yearning for the crunch and crack and crumbling tooth—
to bite down on a secret till it splinters
in the mouth and lodges in the throat like proof.
Lithophagus, at heart, I shrugged at that taboo
and swallowed stonier things, like loneliness and you.

### Echo Finds Her Voice

Nothing new to say about love
or lust—same old, same old
broken heart and ruined dress—
crumpled bed and rumpled nylons
in a pile beside. She gathers them
to her thighs, catches the edge
of the sheer fabric in the garter belt.
Smooths the silk down over her curves,
an unfamiliar sound rising in her throat:
she mutters obscenities into the glass
of spirits held to sweetly bruised lips,
where his beautiful face is mirrored,
her own words returning to her ears
over and over and over again.

### MANY WAYS OF LEAVING

There are many ways
of leaving. Part by part:

head first, like the hound
circling too far afield
to hear the call
and cry of downing dusk,
of chase's end,
the ring of eye and brush
of feathered tail entreating
until the trail is lost and
so is home and hearth;

or blindly, as the heart
when surgeons grope in cavities
for tendril vein and shard
and clot, but with feeling
sheathed against the stain
and blood-borne ill,
the wound is closed
around the weeping,
unseen fatal cut;

or yet, the body leads—
emerging like the moth
from stifling chrysalis,
bent and bruised
but poised
for certain flight
toward some brilliant death;

or leaving simply
for the sake of leaving:
the maverick craving
wild grass more than hay
or grain; the pigeon, homing
back once more,
passes on, then up

into the loss of open sky—
not from, but to

like me to me,
from you.

# MYTH-INFORMATION

*In a time of universal deceit, telling the truth is a revolutionary act.*
—George Orwell

# MYTH INFORMATION

## I.

*I don't mind living in a man's world as long as I can be a woman
in it.*                         —Marilyn Monroe

"How do you find your way back in the dark?"
Marilyn Monroe asks in her last screen shot
on the set of *Something's Got to Give*. Hard
to do, Norma, when what you've got
on your hands is not one but two pretty
boys with full heads of hair and perfect teeth
(not to mention their wives and the secret
service). You emerged on the stage, shimmied
in your shimmery sheath, and purred the tune
they told you to sing. Watched as Narcissus blew
out his candles in the gloom, and too soon
your flame, too, was snuffed. So we will never know
how you felt about dying in that man's world
where the night is littered with your broken pearls.

## II.

*A 41-inch bust and a lot of perseverance will get you more than
a cup of coffee—a lot more.*            —Jayne Mansfield

The night road was littered with broken pearls
and a platinum wig and a little
dog's body or two. Was it true, fiddler girl,
that blondes have more fun, even from the bottle
of peroxide or Miss Clairol? Buxom
nymph, "all pink and cuddly," making a career
of just "being a girl." You saw what you wanted
and got it, didn't you, Jaynie? *Illegal*
as sin, *The Girl Can't Help It*, those double D's
like howitzers in the stunned faces of men,
loosed on a stretcher on U.S. 90,
your loveliness sheared away and smashed in:
they claimed you'd lost your head, sweetheart,
like the world according to Joe McCarthy.

# III.

*The modern champions of communism have selected this as the
time, and ladies and gentlemen, the chips are down — they are
truly down.*                                        —Joseph McCarthy

The world according to Joe McCarthy
was black and white, and red all over
Hollywood; and even of the Army
he asked "Are you now or have you ever
been a Communist?" It is not religion
on which the masses become dull and numb,
that old myth of the Marxists. Suspicion,
implication, and fear are stronger drugs
and easier to swallow when the chips
are down, and maybe the Rosenbergs
really were spies and loose lips do sink ships.
But "Have you no sense of decency, Sir?"
drunk on booze and power, frightened as a girl
of the Communists taking over the world.

# IV.

*They fought like Tigers, but their fight was doomed before the first
man hit the beach.*         —CIA operative Grayston Lynch
*My son is still too young to realize what has happened here. ... It
is my hope that he'll grow into a man at least half as brave as the
members of Brigade 2506.*
                    —Jackie Kennedy, Orange Bowl, 1962

The communists did not take over the world—
but didn't we run them through the muck and mud
of every damn continent, boys? Ensnarled
and engaged in contests where the blood
of peasants and workers flowed in the streets
for being on the side of right and might,
which was ours. Hell, we had to have those cheap
goods from Korea and China, and right
under our noses, Fidel had his showdown
and rattled the rusted bars of his cage,
while the Essex was ordered to stand down
off the shore and the crew watched in tears of rage:
from such hypocrisy and idleness
bomb drills and shelters could never save us.

# V.

*There is also a wider cost, what might be called the moral damage*
*of war.*                                      —Anonymous
*In war, there are no unwounded soldiers.*      —Jose Narosky

Bomb drills and shelters could never save us
from what was coming our way: a handsome
brother who murdered his wife in Corpus
Christi. Newly married, and just arrived home
from Korea, in the middle of the night
he shot her in the back at the Sundown Club
on Poth Lane. A dive no doubt, and why
she was there at 1 a.m. on a Monday? What
can I say? Her name was Bobbie, but just Kay
was all the newspapers said. What went wrong?
Whatever it was, the jury believed. He remained
a hero in blue, his honor intact, strong
and brave. But from such grievance cancers spread:
like nuclear blasts and M & Ms in red.

# VI.

*Most children were only vaguely aware of, or capable of*
*understanding, the fears that may have kept their parents up at*
*night...*                      —Steve Gillon, *Boomer Nation*

Nuclear blasts and M & Ms in red
and mercury from broken thermometers:
everyday dangers to a 1950's kid.
And what about that fluoroscope where mothers
eagerly stuck their children's feet above
a thinly-covered x-ray tube at the shoe store,
to check the fit of Poll Parrots or Buster
Browns, then sent them out to strangers'
porches on Halloween to bring back bags
of apples with embedded razor blades
and poisoned candy from the deviants
they warned the kids about, those guys who sprayed
their places with DDT and wet-dreams
about good girls who had sex in back seats.

# VII.

*If Kinsey is right, I have only done what comes naturally…*
> —Mae West

Good girls did not have sex in back seats
and wouldn't think of using a tampon
or a hula-hoop, those adolescent
sex toys! They sat in rows in darkened rooms
to watch *Girls Beware!* Or stole the copy
of their mother's *Sex Without Fear* hidden
in her drawers, to learn how boys with sloppy
kisses had "Roman hands and Russian Fingers."
And they danced with them at arm's length to prevent
any contact "down there," while bad girls
did the dirty dog in dim lit basements,
grinding their hips and thighs, their skin-tight skirts
hiked up, their round heels, so we were told, spread
for their lovers on their own parents' beds!

# VIII.

*Unwed mothers should be punished and they should be punished*
*by taking their children away.* —Dr. Marion Hilliard,
> Women's College Hospital, 1956

Town girls took their lovers to their own parents' beds
when the boys came home from college on a break—
they smoked and drank and lost their maidenheads
to guys who dated rich coeds back at State
and had no intention of being caught,
laughed it off when "Sister Mister. [Period]"
"Wake up, little Susie!" You'll find you're late
and if you're lucky, you'll be a blushing bride;
alone in a "maternity home for unwed
mothers" if you're not. Return to gossip
about that six-month stay at your "maiden
aunt's" in Peoria or New Haven, a grownup
who weeps in the dark for her baby and her sin.
Was Dr. Spock wrong about discipline?

## IX.

*Yippies, Hippies, Yahoos, Black Panthers, lions and tigers alike
—I would swap the whole damn zoo for the kind of young
Americans I saw in Vietnam.*

                                        —Spiro Agnew

Was Dr. Spock wrong about discipline
and responsible for a generation
out of control? Or was it just coincidence,
those Hippies a decade later, a nation
of free-for-all and free love, covered in mud
at Woodstock, stoned and naked at love-
ins in the parks near Haight and Ashbury? But
there were the others, too, spattered with blood
in Nam, stoned and contaminated with
Agent Orange and nightmares they'd never
forget. Gentle brothers and sons were killed
there although they came back alive, severed
emotions their only mortal wounds, dismissed
as contrary by the psychologists.

## X.

*I didn't want to repeat my parents' life. I saw in their lives a
routine and a lack of dreaming, a lack of the possibilities, a lack
of passion. And I didn't want to live without passion.*

                                        —Hugh Hefner

Contrary to noted psychologist
Wertham, juvenile delinquents did not
just materialize from reading comics.
But something did come up from the sexpot
pin-up mags they found hidden in the liquor
cabinet behind the Scotch their fathers saved
for weak Old Fashioneds after TV dinners
and a stroll outside to watch *Echo* behave
like good girls always do—on cue and primped:
the house work done, dinner cooked, clever
pillow conversation. But naughty nymphs?
Bettie Page, her black bangs and her leather,
showed with her pink-cheeked bum
that a good spanking never hurt anyone.

## XI.

*Truth is like the sun. You can shut it out for a time, but it ain't goin' away.*                                     —Elvis Presley
In 1957, Dr. Arthur Guy Mathews *cures* lesbian by hiring
a fashion expert to teach makeup and hair styling.

A good spanking never hurt anyone:
ubiquitous and varied wooden paddles,
those instruments of painful learning, hung
on leather straps in every classroom. Ankle-
grabbing greasers valued swats like privates
counted stripes on NCOs—a real man
had to take his lumps and be proud of it.
Girls escaped such punishment, but could plan
on kneeling in the office with a too-short skirt,
while smoke-sniffing old maids prowled the toilets.
Parents and teachers listened to experts
back then: Elvis's music would rot your brain, but
it couldn't hurt your eyes looking at an eclipse
and lesbians could still be "cured" with beauty tips.

## XII.

EX-GI BECOMES BLONDE BOMBSHELL!
                    —*Daily News*, December 1, 1952
*Christine Jorgensen went abroad and came home a broad.*
                    —1950's joke

Lesbians can be cured with beauty tips
and homosexuals do not belong;
they should be treated with shock and snips
between the lobes of their brains to right their wrongs.
Ignorance, of course, but still the brilliant fires
in the eyes of the beautiful and queer
were snuffed with scalpels and electrode wires.
So, you have to love a guy who dons a brassiere
and has the balls, so to speak, to be *her*self,
who once had Army privates in the Bronx—
George, until he turned the scalpel on himself.
"There ain't nothin' like a girl," a hirsute debutante
"who can turn the world on with her smiles,"
a Toni, and tube of *Fire and Ice*.

## XIII.

*It was a strange stirring, a sense of dissatisfaction, a yearning*
*that women suffered in the middle of the twentieth century in the*
*United States....the silent question: 'Is this all?'*—Betty Friedan

A Toni and a tube of *Fire and Ice,*
some typing lessons, and a course in shorthand
could take a girl a long way if she was wise—
four years at teachers' college, or white-capped
and smelling of ether and chlorophyll.
But the high-paying factory jobs? "Gone
to soldiers every one..." It's all downhill
my poor, dear Rosie, back in the kitchen
with Dinah and the girls for the next few years,
so Prince Charming's starting to look pretty
good, Princess, when the rent is in arrears
and you're alone in the big, bad city.
Lois had her Clark Kent, but take her advice:
"Superman can't turn this world." He's died twice.

## XIV.

*I look forward to an America which will not be afraid of grace*
*and beauty.*                          —John F. Kennedy
*Fear not the path of truth, fear the lack of people walking on it.*
                          —Robert F. Kennedy

Superman can't turn the world, he's died twice
trying. Those magic bullets were made of lead
and killed like glowing chunks of Kryptonite:
the lovely King of Camelot was dead,
the princely brother soon to lose his crown
as well. And, too, those weavers of the darkest dreams
and brightest hopes fell silent to the southern
soil. "Anybody here seen my good friend, Abraham?
I thought I saw him walking up over the hill..."
to My Lai, and Watergate, past the bare
remains of napalmed jungle and the swill
of ghetto gutters: when hate and warfare
have killed the lights and all the landmarks
how do you find your way back in the dark?

# XV.

*Darkness cannot drive out darkness; only light can do that.*
*Hate cannot drive out hate; only love can do that.*
                              —Martin Luthor King, Jr.

How do you find your way back in the dark
when the road is littered with broken pearls
like the world according to Joe McCarthy:
the communists did not take over the world,
bomb drills and shelters could never save us
from nuclear blasts or even M & M's in red.
Good girls did not have sex in back seats,
they took their lovers to their parents' beds.
Dr. Spock was wrong about discipline:
contrary to noted psychologists
a good spanking never hurt anyone,
and lesbians need not be cured with beauty tips:
a Toni and a tube of *Fire and Ice.*
Superman can't turn this world; he's died twice.

# TRINITY

## I.

*I am become death, the destroyer of worlds.*
*—Bhagavad Gita*, quoted by J. R. Oppenheimer

From a darkness so deep all else is forgotten
spring the words: *I am become Death, the destroyer*
*of worlds*. Six and nine are the same figure—dropped on
its head, nine becomes six. A six-year-old boy or
a nine-year-old girl, or their fathers and mothers,
their siblings, their teachers, the shopkeepers and shops—
their little worlds destroyed, along with the others
in that inferno three full miles across. The drops
of *Little Boy* bomb then *Fat Man* three days later
(August 6th and 9th), did not seek out the soldiers,
but targeted the cities' centers. The greater
to wreak some havoc, the more to smolder
human flesh and dignity. As black water rained,
the unseen enemy knitted its own dark chain.

## II.

*As West and East / In all flatt Maps—and I am one—are*
*one, / So death doth touch the Resurrection.*
*—*John Donne, as quoted by J. R. Oppenheimer

The unseen enemy knitted its own dark chain
of silent destruction across New Mexico
and Nevada, as bombs burst over the plains,
spewing widespread radiation. The blasts echoed
off mountains, while mile-high clouds flashed like the sun
and the toxic green glass glowed, hidden underground
at the Trinity site, where *the gadget* had done
its terrible work upon the innocent sand
and soil for half a country or more, while
generals hid the truth. From West to East they spread—
the lies and results of that terrible work: trying
out the bomb. "Now, we are all sons of bitches," said
Kenneth Bainbridge at the "foul and awesome display"
that marked the beginning: a country's decay.

## III.

*Women and men (both little and small)*
*cared for anyone not at all*
*they sowed their isn't they reaped their same*
*sun moon stars rain*

— e.e. cummings

What marked the beginning of a country's decay
was not just that the danger was already known—
but that old hat trick—deceit, deception, and delay—
the triumvirate of power over drones:
entrenched near ground zero volunteers knelt en masse—
"Put on your goggles," those present were commanded,
"Observers without goggles must face away from the blast"—
then were sent to inspect the destruction first hand:
armless manikins, their clothing scorched and charred,
still standing in rows like dumb sheep to the slaughter
or vaporized sitting in false houses where easy chairs
faced TV screens of deadly snow—fake daughters,
sons, and parents—synthetic stand-ins for the death
that was already rearing its three ghastly heads.

## IV.

*Little Lamb, who made thee?*
*Dost thou know who made thee?*
*Gave thee life, and bid thee feed,*
*By the stream and o'er the mead.*

—William Blake

What was already rearing its three ghastly heads
across innocent arroyos and credulous flats
was the beast whose invisible venom would spread
to east, north, and south. The sheep in their pastures
grazed the valley of death with its grasses so *hot*
that they went to their pens with burned faces and lips.
Then that spring of dead lambs and the miscarried lot,
the deformed, the stillborn, and the too weak to live.
And the sheep that survived sloughed off wool in great clumps,
baring festered blisters. When ranchers complained
of lost dollars and herds, the AEC played dumb
and claimed all was well, so their fears were allayed.
If the Lord was their shepherd, He must have been lost
in the red tape and radioactive exhaust.

## V.

*Who has seen the wind?*
*Neither you nor I:*
*But when the trees bow down their heads*
*The wind is passing by.*

—Christina Rosetti

In the red tape and radioactive exhaust
dispersed by the winds that blew down from the mountains,
from the bomb after bomb detonated out west,
identified dangers disregarded (again
and again and again) freely drifted back East.
They fed orphans oatmeal with radioactive trace
to read the results, tested prisoners' testes
after irradiation, gave "vitamins" laced
with plutonium to expectant mothers
to see what would happen. They knew, they knew, they knew.
But they kept their secrets, denying the others
who were dying or dead from the shadows that grew
in their thyroids and marrow, contaminated
with the evil those "sons of bitches" created.

## VI.

*"We've hunted," sighed Mother,*
*"As hard as we could*
*And I am so afraid that we've*
*Lost him for good."*

—Dorothy Keeley Aldis

The evil those "sons of bitches" created
loomed over the country for a whole generation:
the sirens would shrill, as school children vacated
their desks in a panic, rushed to the foundation
or basement to kneel on the floor, with "Noses to knees!"
while the bombs did *not* fall, but the threat still remained
so that fear was the remedy, fear the disease.
The lucky had shelters dug in their backyards. Planes
would pass over; some knelt in the dirt, terrified
that the bombing had started. Some felt the pressure,
afraid in the end there would be nowhere to hide
like those "human phantoms" from government tests,
where the sick, dead, and dying had been on their minds.
For they knew, they knew, they knew. Repeat it three times.

# VII.

*Batter my heart, three person'd God.*
> —John Donne, as quoted by J. R. Oppenheimer

They knew. They knew. *They knew.* Repeat it three times.
Do not claim they did not know what they were doing.
Do not say the dead were not already on their minds
before the first bomb burst. For a fire storm was brewing
in the hearts of men in power—the knowledge that fear
will seek its own three levels. The first, concealment
and its pale, sickly stepbrother: that great desire
not to know, to go about one's daily life intent
on preservation. Second, that holy vengeance
is delicious on soft white bread, served with white milk
on a white plate of black lies. Lastly, a lusty trance
like that of men in brothels, hypnotized by silk-
clad breasts and thighs—a numb pleasure misbegotten
from a darkness so deep all else is forgotten.

Note: The first nuclear bomb test was conducted on July 16, 1945 in a remote area of New Mexico. J. Robert Oppenheimer gave the project the code name "Trinity," believed to be inspired by the writing of poet John Donne. The informal name of the bomb was "The Gadget." Little more than three weeks after the initial test, on August 6, 1945, an atomic bomb known at "Little Man" destroyed the city of Hiroshima, Japan; three days later "Fat Man" was detonated over Nagasaki, Japan. These three explosions ushered in the Atomic Age.

AEC- Atomic Energy Commission

# Scandal

*Her being a cry to which no echo came or can ever come...*
—Adrienne Rich, "Hunger"

# Assumptions of the Virgin

Cast in light as bright as rococo gilt
that frames and bears her upward
on the crescent moon's silver blade,
El Greco's untouched Virgin rises
from the mouth of opened stone
she's slipped, away from earth and toward
the arch of gold-domed Heaven
where reverential angels wait.

But somewhere along the dim lit hall,
Our Lady of forgotten corners and the unnamed
sculptor—Mary of the marble gaze, Virgin
of the chipped away and what remains—
assumes her stance: arms outstretched
to balance on her shattered toes, time-grimed
face alert as if to catch the crack and crash
of falling stone, the silent rising of the dust.
One wretched cherub crushed beneath her ruined hem.

Note: Based on El Greco's *Assumption of the Virgin* and an anonymous marble
sculpture c. 1700 of the same title, both of which reside not far from one another
at the Art Institute of Chicago.

## SCANDAL

*A woman without humor is a lost woman.*   —Djuna Barnes

Nellie wore *Slightly Wicked* cologne—
the bottle shapely, a deep shade of rose:
that blush from a woman who understands
the bawdy joke, the double entendre—
a knock off ordered from catalogs of household
supplies—brushes, brooms, dust mitts, cleanser—
and delivered by a traveling salesman.
Did he sit there at her sunny table
drinking coffee, nibbling at her cookies?
Would he have smiled at her? She him? So far
from town where her husband struggled
with a wrench, soaked in sweat
and grease, the brash women flaunting their charms
on calendars pinned to auto shop walls
wearing dark ink bikinis and lead gray peignoirs
she had drawn over perfect breasts and perky nipples
to spite her husband and the grimy men
who checked oil, filled radiators, and
lubricated the wheels of the townsfolk.

There is nothing much to tell
of their early years, only a few photos
remain: Buck, lean and tall, leaning
against a fence in black and white,
a pipe to his lips. She, a young woman
dressed in flapper gear—cloche hat
pulled tight over bobbed hair, jazz dress,
turned down stockings—posed
against a summer's trellis heavy with
blooming clematis. Nellie at 29—scandal
the one easy thing for a woman
back then: a young divorcee, marrying
an even younger man. Her prettiness mature,
almost amused, her feet set solidly aground.

In her failing years, she knew death to be
as certain as the final breath he had breathed
in their bedroom that last night; turning back
from the window she had lifted open
at his request she saw that he was gone,
knew she would follow him, but in her own time.
From then, each time she felt a palpitation
of her unsteady heart, she calmly bathed,
donned her prettiest negligee. Then slipped
out on the porch to lounge on the glider,
waiting for death to step lightly through fields

of fescue and foxtails in the valley
along Spoon River, up the hill and past
the cow's barn to claim her. She was found,
not on the farm, but propped up
in a hospital bed, a muslin gown and cawl
of an oxygen tent shrouding the rigor
of her body. Those gray eyes wide open
as if to witness the finder's surprise. The last laugh
and a smear of *Fatal Apple* clinging to her lips.

## THE NINTH MUSE: ANAPHORA FOR CORAZÓN

*It just wasn't their night.*—Murderer Richard Speck

There should have been eight that night.
As there were while he stalked them
coming and going from their studies,
sunning in the park, laughing together.

There should have been eight that night
from the days his heavy-lidded stare bore
through the young men escorting them home,
those men he hated, but envied even more.

There should have been eight that night,
or so he thought as he pressed his way
in through the back door, gun in hand,
knife at the ready, a hunter's cruel heart.

There should have been eight that night,
but there were nine. A hapless friend
visiting on a whim, caught up by fate
in the hell he claimed he was born to raise.

There should have been eight that night.
Corazón—her mother's *heart*, father's *niña*—
rolled beneath the bed, small and unnoticed
because there should have been eight.

There should have been eight that night,
like the muses: *heavenly one, dancer of light,*
*voice of an angel, giver of joy, giver*
*of fame, the festive one, the many-hymned.*

There should have been eight that night:
the eighth, *arouser of desire*, Madonna-
prostitute in his eyes, the only one
he ravaged, left staring, strangled and blue.

There should have been eight that night
but the ninth muse, *Melpomene*, no longer
celebrator of singing and dancing,
listened and watched as all the others disappeared.

There should have been eight that night.
Now the ninth wears heavy boots of woe,
the mask of tragedy in one hand, a knife,
a bloodied knife, in the other. Saved

only because there should have been eight
that night. So the slayer of the fates, silencer
of the muses, confused in the carnage, lost
count, missing the witness, the ninth, the muse

*Melpomene*, who lived to point a finger
and exclaim: "This is the man!" Silenced,
eight others; now the ninth muse sings no more:
holding only her tragic mask, that dripping blade.

Note: On the night of July 13, 1966, Richard Speck forced his way into a townhouse
where eight student nurses were housed, not knowing that a ninth young woman
was visiting. His miscalculation allowed Corazón Amurao to roll beneath a bunk
bed, press against a wall, and remain undetected. It was her description of Speck
(particularly a tattoo that read *Born to Raise Hell*) and subsequent testimony that
brought about his conviction. He died in prison at age 49.

## PANES

Perhaps she sensed him near: that prickle
that skims the skin like a loosed curl
against a bared neck. Some shivering proof
that we are not so removed from animals:
for our fear also has a throb, a scent. Or
did he speak in low tones, come close
and touch her elbow tentatively
like an old friend disremembered,
his face unfamiliar
until she stepped into the cold
glow of the street lamp along the avenue.

Saw the awful truth in his eyes
as he circled away, startled by a beam of light
from a window above where some wife turned down
the narrow bed for her surly husband,
carried a thick blanket to the Davenport
in the dim living room, then lay
down with her ears pressed between pillows,
a cold cloth against her purpling, puffy eye;

a window where a graying woman awoke behind the shades
of her dream about kids' slaughter and nanny goat screams
on a farm long since plowed under by progress,
turned on the bedside lamp to listen,
then lay back staring at shadows
that spread like bloodstains
on the ceiling, remembering her dead father
and her hatred of his assassin's hands,
his impenetrable, stony heart. Like a feral dog

with a taste of flesh from the injured lamb,
the stranger returned again and again
to cut her off from the flock—and not a stab
of guilt from those above, who heard
or watched, pulled back the heavy curtains
at the first cry, let them fall across the paned
glass squared onto the scene,
ears pressed to the window, cold
with March's sudden chill.

While the vile animal played out
his purpose—no clean kill,
but a torturous game, toying with her as men do

in Friday night bars, with lithe smiles
and heavy-lidded eyes. Those weapons
that disarm a girl until she submits
and yields to his rough hands, the hot blade
of his tongue, his rapacious sex, the cold steel
of a morning abandoned. Girls who are the blessed

ones on this spring night. Lucky to weep alone, alive
in the dark, to draw down their simple green
window shades, pull up around their bargained bodies
their grandmother's pieced quilts
brought with them from Cincinnati or Albany.
Her deliberate stitches having sutured
the squared remnants of outgrown girlhood
dresses, school skirts and blouses,
then the sharp needle nicked the heart-
and-flower pattern, piecing
together those worn-soft memories
of an innocence lost.

Note: March 27, 1964—Catherine Genovese was stabbed to death near her home
in New York City while her neighbors watched. According to a *New York Times*
report, the killer made three attacks spread out over more than 30 minutes, during
which 38 people watched. Not one of the bystanders helped the young woman or
called for help, either saying they "didn't want to get involved" or they had been
too afraid to call the police.

# PRIVATE DIRT

*I am not the butcher of Galesburg!*—Dr. Santamaria

He claimed
his wife had disappeared,
that she had long threatened
divorce and leaving him
and their several children.
*He was telling the truth.*

She was gone.
Friends and family had searched,
but the fiery Mexican beauty
was vanished
perhaps run away
with some faceless lover.
He said he didn't know
where she could be.
*He lied.*

The hundreds of cadavers
he had autopsied
stared back at him through
her blank eyes, as he slipped
the skin of his beloved's
face from its bony rack.
He told himself it was
just one more.
No different.
*He lied.*

He dug into the soft
earth of the garden,
as the children learned
geography and math
or slept fitfully, missing
their mother's kisses, planted
the carefully bound bundles.
Was there a plan?

Did sawed-off legs go
next to hacked arms
in some sort of macabre
pattern? Perhaps
he told himself it mattered.
If so, *he lied.*

The raw, wounded
globe, stripped
of every expression
and bound into a tidy
package with twisted,
broken fingers—flailed
flesh hanging,
fingertips gnawed away—
was found buried
in the private dirt
of their cellar.
Didn't know where she was?
*He lied.*

At the service
desk of the local Sears,
Roebuck and Company,
he returned
the carefully washed
and repackaged Cuisinart—
scrubbed clean
of all gristle,
shard and clots.
Said his wife didn't like it.
*He was telling the truth.*

## BLOOD BROTHERS

Her hair, brilliant, but unruly
as her tongue—a comb held up
to settle the waves. Three teeth broken
cleanly away as the bullet flew
through window glass, ricocheted
erratic paths around her skull,
cracking her surprised reflection
in the mantel mirror.

She had come between the lovers
like the Bard's meddlesome nurse:
bitter whispers in the ear
of her friend, a sock hop Juliet.
Reason enough for that Romeo—
side-burned and duck-tailed—
his dark young assassin's face
glowing gray on the tiny screen
in living rooms of respectable citizens.

Forgotten, their two brothers
pass in locker-lined halls—
one blond, thin, the other soft and dark.
Forgetting sometimes
which brother was whose—
the killer's or the victim's—
never meeting the other's eyes,
brothers related only by blood.

In the stifling green classroom,
shades drawn on tall windows
open to the unseasonable heat
of another Illinois autumn,
they sit apart at wooden desks
with strangers' initials carved
in hearts forever entwined.

Note: High school student, Gary Wixforth shot and killed Phyllis Olinger in the early 1960's in an Illinois town. Their brothers were in the same class through junior high and high school.

## BURNING LOVE

*My story is a love story….But only those tortured by love can know what I mean.*                                    —Martha Beck

Ray promised all of them an end
to long nights playing Sinatra and solitaire
at the folding card table,
but the plan sometimes went wrong—
as schemes are wont to do:
*Lonely Hearts* broken
too easily—pulsing bulls eye
of desire for a handsome cupid
to dart with his poison arrow.
A lovelorn woman's hope

grows like malignancy—too rapidly
and without division—one red cell,
irrational and rabid, that envelopes
reason and good sense, eating away
at everything her mother ever warned:
her husband, now dead, never good
enough. Her mother, now dead, and good
riddance—the rest of her life to live
as she pleases. And it pleases her
to no longer be a widow,
but a wife. As it would me:

Martha, the woman who must pretend
*sister* and watch from the shadows
their ignorant cooing and fawning,
their belief that love is flowers
and candy, walks in the snow, fireside
kisses. The fools! *I* had him.
He was *mine*: real love tortures
and flames. The pittance
we stole from stupid women was nothing
compared to what I gave to be his:
easy for me to pull the cordon tighter
around her sagging neck, the skin
creped as ruined silk, aging

eyelids drooped in disgusting death.
Soon enough my own torment
will end. Undying love lives
only as long as life: mine burned
to ruins, heart cooked like nothing
but a cheap piece of meat. Crackling
skin and singed hair sending up,
like some profane penance for love,
the rank stench of my searing devotion.

Note: "[The Lonely Hearts Killers]…Mrs. Beck and [Raymond] Fernandez were
electrocuted for bludgeoning and strangling Janet Fay, 66, an Albany, N.Y., widow,
on Jan. 4, 1949

## Two Sijo IV

### A Star Fell on Alabama

Sylacauga Meteorite: 1954

A small white house just down the block
from Comet Drive-in Restaurant

Ann Hodges resting on a couch
wanting a break from her dull life

She wished she might, she wished she may
She got the wish she wished that day


### I Fall to Pieces

March 5, 1963

You fell among us like a meteor
a sweet dreamer with crimson lips

Your velvet voice, singed with sorrow
like a lovely flame going out

At the crash site, a final song
your red slip hanging in a tree

### ELEGY FOR SALLY AND ROSE

Alderson Women's Prison, West Virginia

Speak to me, sisters, as we pass in the yard.
Speak to me in the words of freedom,
of liberty as you saw it. Look me in the eye
and tell me it was worth it, whatever it was—
an ideal, a man, a roof overhead and a meal.

Remember the power your voices held, how men
would listen when you spoke, your mouths warm
with seditious honey, your tongues fascinating
as serpents' forks with the lies they feared.
But every man adores a spy—his mother
asking questions of the stained handkerchief,
his little woman watching the clock till dawn,
waiting for the whiskey breath and alibi.
What woman would not want to be you?

And what woman could not fear you, safe
in her house-dressed world, considering you,
dangerous in numbered khaki. Remember,
we are all at the work of women on their hands
and knees, scrubbing the dirt of life from a floor
we have not soiled, wiping away the wet stains
of sex from our bodies and beds. It is woman's
place, you know, to sow where she will not reap,
sew the things she will not wear, and be thankful

to clean up the mess afterward. A jury of your
true peers—trusting women, misled, led on,
turned down, knocked up, abused, and abandoned—
would have found you guilty as traitors to no one
but yourselves. Caged, a lark refuses to sing
but a few broken chords remembered from her
freedom. Sing, my sisters, sing. You are us.
We hear your voices echoing through the tunnel,
reverberating from the cell block to solitary.

Note: Mildred Gillars (aka "Axis Sally") and Iva Toguri (aka "Tokyo Rose") were
both imprisoned at Alderson Women's Prison from 1949 to 1956, when
Toguri was released. Toguri was later pardoned by President Gerald Ford in
1977, on his last day in office.

## CONFESSION

*There is no love that is not an echo.*     —Theodor Adorno

## SOCIAL STUDIES

These hills with flashing, rock bound streams are not my home,
        no matter that I call them mine now:
        these miles of white-fenced pastures,
        paddocks rife with manure's oath,
        black barns with red doors open
                on leathered leaves of slow death,
        these risings and declines of earth—
                evidence of the glaciers push and pull.

No matter that I've braved the granite coast, breathed the rockweed salt;
        no matter my love beneath magnolias (with amends to pansies
        planted in December) under Carolina blue.
It may be true: *You can never go home*; but truer is this:
                home can never go from you—
        my land is squared by pavements' blades, harrowed into shape,
        flat page of an atlas, the story told between the fence lines:

I am from soybeans' low bustle; the gossip of tall corn,
        silks growing brittle in the heavy, heat-infused wind,
        rasp of leaves against young skin, marking me as its own
        wherever I go; harsh whispers before a storm,
                and the listening ears.

I am from dark clouds sweeping East across the plains:
        from the safety found beneath school room desks,
                against hallway lockers, hands over heads:
                threats of tornadoes, communists, and bombs,
        from lightning strikes, burning barns, thunder threatened
                and delivered: a president—young and beautiful—
                dead on the small gray screen.

I am from the clear shallows of Spoon River, deep in the valley
                of my uncle's farm:
        from shiners and crawdads, minnows in glass jars, and arrowheads—
                pointed truths—prized only for their ease of being found;
        from the dust of summer hayloft and the scrabble of mice
                in autumn corn crib—I am lifted
        from wavy-edged Kodacolor in my cowboy hat and mud-caked boots.

I am silk purses from sows' ears; pearls before swine:
        from my brother's outgrown parka and toboggan
                on sled rides down Secord's hill,
        from feed sack blouses and handed down skirts—
                out of style, but sturdy—my first bra
        from a box of cousin's cast-offs,
from one pair of shoes to wear every day of eighth grade:
                hated and red as pride.

I am from a Sweden my father never spoke of because he never learned
                the language of his father:
        from names like Ola, Elna, Orlo, Olaf;
        from *gudda flicka*, and St. Lucia Day—
                my mother's crown of light in the winter dark—
        from the Baltic Sea where my grandmother ate that good fish
                before she boarded the *Industry* one hundred twenty years ago
                to bring herself to become my namesake, my saint.

I am from my mother's garden—her black Irish rose, Barefoot,
                high-arched, and proud;
        from tea leaves read on lightless winter nights, the drift of vapor rising
        from thin cups like some profane prayer;
        from her father, fallen to the hard life of tenant farming and influenza;
        from Mary, my mother's mother—deaf and ancient—
                born when Lincoln lived, leaving me
                just one generation from the Civil War;
        from North and South, gray against blue like storm clouds
                against a summer sky, my face against my mother's neck,
                hiding from the dead I loved.

I am from stories told—*the truth whether I know it or not*—and graves
                like small, quiet houses visited year after year:
        from an aunt gone insane from syphilis, the knife she raised
                to her own children,
        from her "no good" husband;
        from Little Eva—tiny Ophelia—drowned by her father's hand, and
        from the visions of her that invaded my childhood sleep;
        from Merrill, blood brother I never knew,
                his ghostly highchair not yet empty
                when I was pushed to the table ten years later.

I am from a music that is out of cadence, out of step, out of time, but mine still:
     from "Daddy's Little Girl," "Tennessee Waltz," "Honeysuckle Rose,"
     from "I'll Remember You, Love, in My Prayers" and "Gypsy Davey,"
     from my brothers picking and singing in the small, bright kitchen—
     from the high lonesome they sang and, through them,
     from Hank and Patsy and all who love in vain—those rhythms I carry
          in my head, in my words and lines,
          in my own singing—
          here, today.

## CONFESSION

*Poetry ought to have a mother as well as a father.*
> —Virginia Woolf

Dear Mother, here is my confession:
it is to you I owe my breath and blood.
You were my source and, however
bleak my droughts of soul may be,
yours was the flood that rushed
me, drowned and gasping for air,
onto the shores of this existence.
For what you gave, I thank you
where you now lay— that graveyard
of black gumbo soil, dark and rich
with memories—among your kind:
solid as stones set firmly into prairie earth.

But Mother, there have been others:
those whose words burst open
and bore me, fragile and futile,
into a new life, just as surely as your body—
that precious wound a gate swinging open
one last time for me. I admit there are some
whose lines and phrases slipped as easily
across my lips as that thin liquid
from your cracked and bleeding nipples,
my insistent tugging leaving neither emptied,
both full—those bottomless miracles
of mother's milk, of dreamer's ink.

My cold, sweet Clara, you rest now
so far away from where I lay me down
to sleep among those mothers never dead,
but always waiting with cracked spines,
worn faces of their pages spotted with age
and tears—my own and theirs. I conjure them
by name: *Amy, Elizabeth, Emily, Jane,*
*Muriel, Sylvia, Gwendolyn, Grace.*
Tender and tough, we reason together
of the line, the turn, the image that burns
and sings, those perfect words: *child,*
*daughter,* a library of *mothers.*

## WRITING HISTORY

*I don't know why you chose the path you took.* —My mother.
The last thing she wrote to me before her death at 97.

Looking back at things
to come from a time
not yet arrived,
penning remembrances
of events unfolding
in that future moment
on paper still a tree:

my mother's face
across time,
the lines deeper as I draw
my hand away—
imprinted on my palm,
I read my future there.

## ABOUT THE AUTHOR

A native Mid-Westerner, Christina Lovin was born in Galesburg, Illinois, but has lived and worked in states as varied as Indiana, Ohio, Maine, and North Carolina. She now makes her home in Central Kentucky, where she lives with four rescue dogs in a town reminiscent of Mayberry RFD. After having several careers, including minister's wife, retail shop owner, and VISTA volunteer, she received a Master of Fine Arts in Creative Writing degree from New England College in 2004. She began teaching college-level writing courses that fall, and is currently a full-time lecturer in the English & Theatre Department at Eastern Kentucky University.

Lovin's writing has appeared in over one hundred different literary journals and anthologies, as well as four other volumes of poetry (*A Stirring in the Dark, Flesh, Little Fires,* and *What We Burned for Warmth*). She is the recipient of numerous poetry awards, writing residencies, fellowships, and grants, most notably the Al Smith Fellowship from Kentucky Arts Council and Elizabeth George Foundation Grant. *Echo*, her fifth book of poetry was also generously funded by the Kentucky Foundation for Women.

**ACKNOWLEDGMENTS** Continued

"Myth Information," *Anthropology & Humanism*; "Myth Information" (excerpt), *Stimulus Respond;* "Panes"*, *Carried Away* and *Poetry Quarterly* and *Women Write Resistance*; "Paper Doll Ghazal"*, *Collecting Life: Poets on Objects Known & Imagined;* "Pound"*, *Calliope*; "Princess," *Cliterature*; "Private Dirt," *Scalped*; "Roller Rink on a Saturday Night," *Multi-Culti Mixerations*; "Shells," *Extinguished and Extinct*; "Scandal," *Public Republic*; "Slow Burn"*, *Alehouse* and *Escape Into Life*; "Someone Else's Sin"*, *Cliterature;* "Summer '68," *Crab Orchard Review*; "The Mourning After," *Not a Muse* (Haven Books, Hong Kong); "The Other Sister"*, *Naugatuck River Review*; "The Ninth Muse: Anaphora for Corazón"*, *Naugatuck River Review*; "Tooth for a Tooth," *Ab Ovo*; "Trinity," *Stimulus Respond*; "What the Other Woman Knows: haiku to be read alone," *Under the Banana Tree*; "Where Things Came From"*, *Naugatuck River Review*; *"Your Lifetime in Pictures"*, *Stimulus Respond.*

*Poems marked thus also appeared in the chapbook, *Flesh*, published by Finishing Line Press (2013).

In gratitude to Kentucky Arts Council, Kentucky Foundation for Women, and Elizabeth George Foundation for support of my work. With appreciation to Vermont Studio Center, Virginia Center for the Creative Arts, Prairie Center for the Arts, Spring Creek Project, Friends of Connemara, Devil's Tower Writers, and the National Park Service for providing time and space to work on these poems. Special thanks to all my poet and writer friends for critique, counsel, and camaraderie: you know who you are.

# RECENT BOOKS BY BOTTOM DOG PRESS

## BOOKS IN THE HARMONY SERIES

*Echo: Poems*
By Christina Lovin, 114 pgs. $16
*Stolen Child: A Novel*
By Suzanne Kelly, 338 pgs. $18
*The Canary : A Novel*
By Michael Loyd Gray, 196 pgs. $18
*On the Flyleaf: Poems*
By Herbert Woodward Martin, 106 pgs. $16
*The Harmonist at Nightfall: Poems of Indiana*
By Shari Wagner, 114 pgs. $16
*Painting Bridges: A Novel*
By Patricia Averbach, 234 pgs. $18
*Ariadne & Other Poems*
By Ingrid Swanberg, 120 pgs. $16
The Search for the Reason Why: New and Selected Poems
By Tom Kryss, 192 pgs. $16
*Kenneth Patchen: Rebel Poet in America*
By Larry Smith, Revised 2nd Edition, 326 pgs. Cloth $28
*Selected Correspondence of Kenneth Patchen,*
Edited with introduction by Allen Frost, Paper $18/ Cloth $28
*Awash with Roses: Collected Love Poems of Kenneth Patchen*
Eds. Laura Smith and Larry Smith
With introduction by Larry Smith, 200 pgs. $16

## HARMONY COLLECTIONS AND ANTHOLOGIES

*d.a.levy and the mimeograph revolution*
Eds. Ingrid Swanberg and Larry Smith, 276 pgs. $20
*Come Together: Imagine Peace*
Eds. Ann Smith, Larry Smith, Philip Metres, 204 pgs. $16
*Evensong: Contemporary American Poets on Spirituality*
Eds. Gerry LaFemina and Chad Prevost, 240 pgs. $16
*America Zen: A Gathering of Poets*
Eds. Ray McNiece and Larry Smith, 224 pgs. $16
*Family Matters: Poems of Our Families*
Eds. Ann Smith and Larry Smith, 232 pgs. $16

**Bottom Dog Press, Inc.**
PO Box 425/ Huron, Ohio 44839
Order Online at:
http://smithdocs.net/BirdDogy/BirdDogPage.html

# RECENT BOOKS BY BOTTOM DOG PRESS

### BOOKS IN THE WORKING LIVES SERIES

*An Act of Courage: Poems* By Mort Krahling,
Eds. Judy Platz and Brooke Horvath, 104 pgs. $16
*Story Hour & Other Stories*
By Robert Flanagan, 122 pgs. $16
*Sky Under the Roof: Poems*
By Hilda Downer, 126 pgs. $16
*Breathing the West: Great Basin Poems*
By Liane Ellison Norman, 80 pgs. $16
*Smoke: Poems* By Jeanne Bryner, 96 pgs. $16
*Maggot : A Novel* By Robert Flanagan, 262 pgs. $18
*Broken Collar: A Novel* By Ron Mitchell, 234 pgs. $18
*American Poet: A Novel*
By Jeff Vande Zande, 200 pgs. $18
*The Pattern Maker's Daughter: Poems*
By Sandee Gertz Umbach, 90 pages $16
*The Way-Back Room: Memoir of a Detroit Childhood*
By Mary Minock, 216 pgs. $18
*The Free Farm: A Novel* By Larry Smith, 306 pgs. $18
*Sinners of Sanction County: Stories*
By Charles Dodd White, 160 pgs. $17
*Learning How: Stories, Yarns & Tales*
By Richard Hague, 216 pgs. $18
*Strangers in America: A Novel*
By Erika Meyers, 140 pgs. $16
*Riders on the Storm: A Novel*
By Susan Streeter Carpenter, 404 pgs. $18
*The Long River Home: A Novel*
By Larry Smith, 230 pgs. Paper $16/ Cloth $22
*Landscape with Fragmented Figures: A Novel*
By Jeff Vande Zande, 232 pgs. $16
*The Big Book of Daniel: Collected Poems*
By Daniel Thompson, 340 pgs. Paper $18/ Cloth $22;
*Reply to an Eviction Notice: Poems*
By Robert Flanagan, 100 pgs. $15
*An Unmistakable Shade of Red & The Obama Chronicles*
By Mary E. Weems, 80 pgs. $15
*Our Way of Life: Poems* By Ray McNiece, 128 pgs. $15

**Bottom Dog Press, Inc.**
PO Box 425/ Huron, Ohio 44839
Order Online at:
http://smithdocs.net/BirdDogy/BirdDogPage.html

CPSIA information can be obtained at www.ICGtesting.com
Printed in the USA
LVOW06s0947250114

370963LV00002B/35/P